every teenager's
little black book
on sex and dating

by blaine bartel

every teenager's
little black book
on sex and dating

by blaine bartel

Harrison House
Tulsa, Oklahoma

09 08 07 06   20 19 18 17 16 15 14 13 12

Every Teenager's Little Black Book on Sex and Dating
ISBN 1-57794-456-9
Copyright © 2002 by Blaine Bartel
P.O. Box 691923
Tulsa, Oklahoma 74179

Published by Harrison House, Inc.
P.O. Box 35035
Tulsa, Oklahoma 74153

contents

contents (continued)

contents (continued)

Love vs. Lust: Winning the Battle

Happily Ever After

[DEFINING DATING]

3 THINGS DATING IS NOT

Dating is not really a biblical word at all. That doesn't mean it's wrong to go out with someone on a "date." But it is important to remember what the Bible has to say about developing romantic friendships. If you begin dating without some clear guidelines and boundaries, you are headed for disaster.

Let's start by taking a quick glance at what dating is not.

1. **Dating is not for those who aren't ready.** In my opinion, dating shouldn't even be a consideration until a young person is at least 16 years old. That's been "the law" with my 3 teenage boys, and they're doing just fine with it. That doesn't mean you can't have good friendships with the opposite sex; just keep things in a group environment.

2. **Dating is not a great way to "really get to know someone."** Why? Because everyone is on best behavior during a date. If you really want to get to know someone, watch the person at school every day, or both of you get a job together at McDonald's. Eight straight hours over a hot greaser full of fries will tell you the real tale.

3. **Dating is not all it's cracked up to be.** Think about 2 people out together who hardly know each other. They're young and have limited social skills. They have to try to create awkward conversation for hours on end. The point is, it's usually a whole lot easier to get to know someone among a group of other friends who can help fill those awkward moments, keeping things fun.

3 WAYS CHRISTIAN DATING IS DIFFERENT

The world's idea of dating is dangerous at best. That's why the Scripture tells us not to be conformed to this world, but to be transformed by the renewing of our minds. (Rom. 12:2.) We renew our minds with the knowledge of God's Word.

Here are 3 ways a Christian dating experience should be different from one in the world.

1. In the world, people date to check someone out; a Christian date is focused on building someone up. Dating in the world is like "trying someone on" like a pair of shoes—if they don't fit quite right for you, just disregard them and move on to someone else. A Christian's focus should be on encouraging each other in life and in one another's walk with God.

2. The world bases a large part of success in their dates on connecting physically, while Christians should be prizing spiritual things first. It's not that you shouldn't be attracted to someone by looks, but maintaining sexual purity must be at the top of your commitment to each other.

3. The world will often lie and deceive to achieve their goals in dating. Christians are to be committed to integrity and honesty. Don't try to be someone you are not. Tell the truth. If someone doesn't like the "real you," don't worry about it. Obviously, that person isn't "the one."

3 UNCOMMON THINGS
EVERY GIRL WANTS IN A GUY

King Solomon said that a good man is 1 in 1000 and a good woman is nearly impossible to find. (Eccl. 7:28.) So guys, if you want to be that 1 in 1000, you can separate yourself from the pack by living up to these 3 uncommon characteristics.

1. **A spirit of desire.** Proverbs 21:25 says that the desire of a lazy man kills him. Girls are looking for young men who have vision, drive, and desire for life and are willing to work to reach their goals.

2. **A spirit of kindness.** Proverbs 19:22 tells us that kindness is what is desired in a good man. Learn proper etiquette and manners in the way you should treat people.

3. **A spirit of justice.** A just person is someone who has learned to distinguish right from wrong and is not afraid to stand up for truth. Don't back down to the pressure of friends to do wrong or compromise. Have some backbone and be counted.

3 UNCOMMON THINGS
EVERY GUY WANTS IN A GIRL

All right, ladies, turnabout is fair play. You have some expectations too. In a world that has become increasingly corrupt and vulgar, you can stand above the crowd by the way you choose to live. Anyone can follow the masses, but it will be the few who do the right thing who are exalted, promoted, and blessed with the best relationships and a bright future.

What does a real man want in a girl?

1. **Devotion.** A real man will chase a girl who chases after God and is unwilling to compromise and give in to the world. Be devoted to Christ and devoted to His plans for your life. Guys will follow!

2. **Wisdom.** Knowledge is the acquiring of facts and information. Wisdom knows what direction to go with those facts and information. Guys search for a young woman who has the ability to discern and make good decisions.

3. **Encouragement.** Throughout the Bible, we are instructed to encourage one another, inspiring others with our words and good works. Learn to build people

up, not tear them down. A man needs a woman who believes in him and will be a regular source of strength and encouragement.

4 SIGNS THAT YOU
MAY NOT BE READY TO DATE

Okay, you are at a new stage in your life. You have this attraction to the opposite sex that just wasn't there when you were 7 years old and still playing on the swing set in the backyard. Just because you have this new desire for romance doesn't mean it's time to date. Navigating through the complicated world of boy-girl relationships is like learning to fly a 747 jet. You need lots of instruction, preparation, and maturity before you try to take off.

Here are 4 signs that you may want to wait a while before you get your engines going.

1. **Your parents feel you are too young.** Unless you are out of the house, 27 years old, and have a mom and dad who just can't let go, listen to them. They have been down the road you're on.

2. **You have a significant problem with lust.** If you are struggling with pornography and lack control in your thought life, conquer this area first. (2 Tim. 2:21-22.)

3. **God is not first in your life and priorities.** A strong commitment to Christ is the foundation for any good relationship.

4. **You believe dating will finally make you happy and fulfilled.** People are not your answer. If you look to them for your hope and fulfillment, they can quickly become another one of your problems. Only Jesus Christ can fill you with a love that will take away that empty void.

[FRIENDSHIP BEFORE

ROMANCE]

5 WAYS TO ATTRACT NEW FRIENDS

Lee Iacocca says, "Success comes not from what you know, but from who you know and how you present yourself to each of those people."[1] Good friendships are vital to success. Maybe you are in need of some good friends.

Here are 5 ways to attract new friends.

1. **Smile.** Turn that frown upside down. This gesture may be small, but it packs a powerful punch. Showing those pearly whites is a magnet to new friends (be sure those pearls are white). (Prov. 18:24.)

2. **Listen.** Let others talk about themselves, then respond. When someone else is talking, don't be thinking about what you're going to say. Give the person your ear and thoughts. (Prov. 17:28.)

3. **Be dependable.** Be there for others during the good and the bad. Anyone can be there for the fun times, but only a friend will be there when things get rough.

4. **Keep your word.** If you say you are going to do something, do it. Keep your word even if you don't feel like it. If you can't keep a promise, then don't

make it. It's better to under-promise and overachieve. (Prov. 11:3.)

5. **Help others succeed.** Be others-minded. Ask yourself, "How can I help this person?" Then do something about it. If you have this mindset, you will attract so many friends you won't know what to do.

3 FRIENDSHIP KILLERS YOU MUST AVOID

Good friends are hard to come by, and acquiring good friends is only half the battle. The other half is keeping them. If you want to keep your friends, I suggest you don't do these friendship killers.

1. **Gossip.** Gossip is simply mischievous talk about the affairs of others. Proverbs 16:28 says that a gossip separates close friends. A good friend will keep what he or she knows in confidence, unless someone in authority needs to be notified.

2. **Selfishness.** How can we expect to keep the company of others if we are only concerned about ourselves? In Philippians 2:3, Paul wrote that we are to consider others better than ourselves. If we act unselfishly, we will encourage our friendships to grow.

3. **Unforgiveness.** Our friends will make mistakes. Why? Because they are human. As our friends miss it and then turn from their mistakes or sin, we are to forgive them. We are to forgive our friends as Christ forgave us. (Eph. 4:31,32.)

5 THINGS REAL FRIENDS
NEVER DO TO EACH OTHER

If you want to be a real friend, I suggest you do the complete opposite of these 5 things.

1. **Lie and deceive.** A real friend looks out for the interest of others. We must realize that to lie and deceive does not protect anyone, but it hurts all parties involved. Be a person of truth and honesty.

2. **Spread rumors.** Be sure you are a positive promoter for your friends, not a negative rumor spreader. If you're talking bad about someone else, someone else is probably talking bad about you.

3. **Be jealous.** Love is not jealous. (1 Cor. 13:4.) We should be the happiest people our friends know when they succeed. If your friend gets a new video game system, don't be jealous. Enjoy the benefits of your friendship.

4. **Discourage.** Discouragement is simply the taking away of courage. Encourage—give your friends the

courage to face all opportunities and obstacles that come their way. Be your friend's number-one fan.

5. **Give up.** Jesus is our ultimate example of a real friend. Are you thankful He never gave up on us? As a real friend, you shouldn't quit on your friends because of challenging times. Jesus said He would never leave us or forsake us. Let's make that commitment as well.

3 REASONS FRIENDSHIP IS
MORE IMPORTANT THAN ROMANCE

Romance is a good thing. As a married man, I know. However, *friendship* is more important: it should be the foundation that romance is built on. Let's take a look at 3 reasons friendship is more important than romance.

1. **Longevity.** Friendship is long-lasting. Romance is temporary. Romance is defined as a strong, usually short-lived, attachment or feeling. Friendship is there for the long haul.

2. **Not a feeling.** It's a fact. The feeling of romance will come and go. Romance has a lot to do with its environment and circumstances. Friendship, on the other hand, is there whether we feel it or not.

3. **You can be yourself.** You don't have to worry about impressing others. There is no need for you to present yourself in an unrealistic manner to gain affection. A true friend will still love you when you've had one too many Big Macs.

6 FRIENDS THAT ARE NOT
TRUE FRIENDS AT ALL

We have all been in relationships in which we thought someone was our friend and then down the road realized he or she wasn't a true friend. A true friend doesn't just call themself a friend, but backs up his or her words with action. Here are 6 "friends" to avoid.

1. **The back-stabber.** This is someone who acts one way in front of you, but acts totally different behind your back. A back-stabber cannot be trusted by anyone.

2. **The user.** The user is just looking for a temporary friend. This person will borrow your friendship for personal gain and then toss you like a dirty dishrag.

3. **The control freak.** "It's my way or the highway," this one will say. The control freak will not compromise. You're only going and doing what this person wants to do. Your opinion doesn't matter.

4. **The manipulator.** If you don't want to do what the manipulator wants you to do, this person will find a way to convince you to do it his or her way. The

manipulator is sly and will influence you to do things you never thought you would do—all for his or her own selfish ambitions.

5. **The moocher.** This person wants you to provide for his or her every need. "Can I borrow your clothes?" "Can I borrow your car?" "Can I borrow a couple of bucks?" As you give, you'll never receive anything in return. In plain English, this person is a bum.

6. **The complainer.** You can never please the complainer no matter what you do. If you gave this person a $100 bill, he or she would complain because it's not 2 $50 bills. Save yourself and avoid this one.

[BEING THE RIGHT PERSON]

5 KEY CHARACTERISTICS
OF THE RIGHT PERSON

Are you the right person? Are you the man for the job? Are you the woman who will not compromise? We all want that right job, car, spouse, future, or opportunity. For those things to come our way, each of us must first be the right person.

You can begin now to develop these 5 key characteristics of the right person.

1. Integrity is one of the most important characteristics that anyone could have. The right person is the same no matter whom one is with, what one is doing, or where one is. Image is not everything; integrity is. In the end, your life is about being, not appearing.

2. The second key characteristic of the right person is humility. Proverbs 16:18 NIV says, "Pride goes before destruction, a haughty spirit before a fall." You cannot live a life of destruction and expect to be or find the right person. So humble yourself under God's Word by honoring and obeying His direction.

3. Everyone should have an ongoing desire to grow, no matter if it's to get good grades, find a spouse, or

receive a promotion. A desire to grow will help you get there. Keep in mind that the proof of a desire to grow is the pursuit of that desire.

4. Self-control is the fourth key characteristic of the right person. The right person has an understanding that he cannot do everything he "feels" like doing. If it were up to most of us, we wouldn't even get out of bed half the time. As you are on that road to becoming the right person, you must gain control of what that person does.

5. The last characteristic is friendliness. It almost sounds too easy, but this characteristic will take you a long way. No one wants to be around unfriendly people. Think about it. If you went to a restaurant and the food was good but your server was a rude, unfriendly jerk, you would probably think twice before making this the "right" restaurant. Remember to keep in mind the importance of being a friendly person.

3 WAYS TO GUARD YOUR THOUGHT LIFE

Protection. We guard our home, car, skin, and even time, but sometimes we neglect to guard one of the most important areas—our thought life. We need to place a guard over our thought life.

Here's how:

1. **Take control.** Don't allow your thoughts to wander like an out-of-control car. Grab hold of the steering wheel. The Word of God says to take captive every thought and to bring it into the obedience of Christ. (2 Cor. 10:5.) You may not be able to control every thought that comes in, but you can determine whether or not it stays.

2. **Guard your gate.** What's the gate of your mind? It's your eyes and ears. Don't put junk into your thought life by throwing open the gate. Filter what comes in. Remember the computer term G.I.G.O.: garbage in, garbage out.

3. **Thought replacement.** When thoughts of fear or doubt come your way, replace them with love and faith.

You cannot have 2 complete thoughts in your mind at the same time. For good thought replacement ideas, see Philippians 4:8.

3 STRATEGIES TO CONQUER PEER PRESSURE

Satan wants you to lose. His plan is for you to be the wrong person, not the right person. One of his most common tactics is using people around us to influence us in a negative way. That negative influence is what we call peer pressure. The good news is that we can implement 3 practical strategies to conquer peer pressure.

1. **Have good friends.** If you have friends who don't compromise in their Christian beliefs, it will help you to do the same. First of all, they won't ask you to do things they believe are morally wrong. Second, they will help you be accountable for your actions.

2. **Have a predetermined reaction.** In other words, know how you would respond in a particular situation. How would you react if someone tried to influence you in a negative way? It's a lot easier to respond when you already have your mind made up.

3. **Avoid compromising situations.** If you are trying to lose weight, the last place you want to get a job is the chocolate factory. The best way to conquer peer pressure is to avoid it as much as possible.

6 QUESTIONS YOU MUST ANSWER RIGHT

Questions are everywhere–from your little brother to your final exams at school. Without questions we couldn't have answers. Questions help to bring about truth.

If you want to be the right person, you must answer the following questions right.

1. If I were to ask Jesus, "Should I be doing this," would He say yes?

2. Are my actions and words affecting my future and the future of my loved ones in a positive way?

3. If my thought life were to be shown at the local movie theatre, would I invite my parents to watch?

4. If my actions and words were broadcast on the 5:00 news, would I be embarrassed?

5. Have I spent quality time with God today?

6. Is this relationship in my life helping me or hindering me?

4 DANGER ZONES IN
MODERN ENTERTAINMENT

I enjoy good entertainment just as much as the next guy, but I believe that we all must guard the gates of our minds and hearts. Second Timothy 3:1-6 says we are to have nothing to do with wicked and ungodly people. This biblical principle also applies to our entertainment.

Here are 4 danger zones that we must steer clear of in modern entertainment.

1. **Sexual immorality.** The Word of God says that there should not even be a hint of sexual immorality in our lives. (Eph. 5:3.) Have the courage not to compromise even when everyone else will.

2. **Disrespect for authority.** Honoring and obeying our parents will bring us blessings. (Ex. 20:12.) Paul wrote that our police, military, and government leaders are ministers of God. (Rom. 13:6.)

3. **Mocking of God.** Did you know that when you fail to react to others' degrading of God and godly principles, you come into agreement with those acts? Jesus said

that if you're ashamed of Him and the Word, He will be ashamed of you. (Luke 9:26.)

4. **Rage.** Don't believe that uncontrolled anger will bring a solution to your problem. It won't. It will add to your already existing problems. Proverbs 14:16 NIV says, "A fool is hotheaded and reckless." Don't be a fool.

[FINDING THE RIGHT PERSON]

4 REASONS NOT TO TRY TOO HARD

There are times when you can try too hard to get something you really want. I have seen this more often in relationships than in any other area. We must learn to be patient for God's plan for our lives to develop in His timetable, not ours.

Here are 3 reasons not to try too hard to find the one you're looking for.

1. **Trying too hard and pushing too fast will result in a relationship with the wrong person.** Often, if you're trying too hard, you take the first person who comes along.

2. **Others will perceive you as desperate.** This will naturally repel people from you, and you may miss God's best.

3. **Trying too hard shows a lack of faith in God.** Hebrews 11:6 says that we can't please God without faith and faith believes God will reward those who diligently seek Him. Don't seek after relationships. Seek God, and the right relationships will come.

4. **You can go broke.** If you become a "serial dater," you're going to take a major hit in your wallet, especially if you're a guy. This may be a bit on the practical side, but it's still true.

5 KEYS TO KEEP CHRIST FIRST

If we seek to save our lives, we will lose them; but if we lose our lives for Christ's sake, we will find them. (Luke 17:33.) This is somewhat of a paradox, but it is absolutely the truth. It's only when we truly allow Jesus to take all the controls of our lives that things will really take off in the right direction.

Here are 5 keys to keeping Christ first.

1. **Fill your mind with good, life-giving information.** The Bible, good books, and edifying music are just some of the things that can help keep your focus on the Lord.

2. **Pray regularly.** Make God your best friend, not the heavenly rescue team that you only call on when you're in trouble.

3. **Keep good Christian friends.** Proverbs 13:20 says that the companion of fools will be destroyed. Avoid the fools.

4. **Stay committed to your local church.** Christians are unable to survive alone. We are called to be

connected to the Body of Christ in a local church. Go every week, and get involved.

5. **Get rid of sin and weights.** Hebrews 12:1 teaches us that if we want to finish the race God has called us to run, we must lay aside our sin and the weights that may hold us back. You know if there's something holding you back. Leave it behind.

4 DANGER SIGNS TO WATCH
FOR IN THE WRONG PERSON

The Bible warns us not to be unequally yoked together with unbelievers. (2 Cor. 6:14.) The word "yoke" means to be bound together in commitment to one another. When 2 animals are yoked together, when one turns left, the other has to turn left too. It is critical that you walk with people who are going in the right direction.

Here are some flashing warning signs that you may be hanging out with the wrong person.

1. Your conversation always turns away from spiritual things. Those who are really living for Christ will not be ashamed to talk about it.

2. The person is not clear on his or her standards and convictions. If you are with someone who never seems to have an opinion on what is right or what is wrong—DANGER.

3. All of the person's other friends seem to be people who compromise and are not really serving God. This is a dead giveaway that the person is heading down a different road than you want to be on.

4. The person's claim to "believe in God" rarely produces any actions to back it up. The Bible says even the devil believes in God (James 2:19)—so obviously "just believing" is not enough.

7 CRUCIAL QUALITIES YOU MUST FIND

Proverbs 31:10 NKJV asks the question "Who can find a virtuous wife [or husband, for that matter]? For her [or his] worth is far above rubies." This statement confirms the fact that if you are going to find the right person, you are going to have to look very hard to find virtuous qualities.

Here are 7 characteristics you must put on the top of your list.

1. **The person must be born again.** It is not enough to go to church; a virtuous person really is saved and serving God.

2. **The person must have a commitment to sexual purity.** They must have had this commitment before you showed up—not *because* you showed up.

3. **The person must be truthful and honest.** If a person lies to you about small things, he or she will lie to you about the big things one day.

4. **The person must be able to control his or her tongue.** If slander, gossip, or foul language are a normal part of a person's vocabulary, back off.

5. **The person must honor authority.** (Isa. 1:19.) A person who has a rebellious attitude towards those in leadership is headed for destruction.

6. **The person must hate sin.** Proverbs 8:13 says to fear God and hate evil. Does this person?

7. **The person must respect you.** Does this person treat you with dignity, purity, honor, and respect? If not, move on.

3 THINGS THEY DON'T TELL
YOU ABOUT EVERY PERSON

In your quest to find Mr. or Mrs. Right, I've got a flashing piece of revelation for you. You're never going to find someone who is perfect in all he or she does. What you want to find is someone who has a "perfect heart." A perfect heart will quickly make changes and adjustments after sinning or making mistakes.

Locate someone with a heart after God and remember these 3 things.

1. Every person has certain "personality quirks" that may rub you the wrong way sometimes. Maybe he or she is not really organized or takes forever to make a point when talking. Work with the person.

2. Every person is going to find some things in you that he or she doesn't like. In fact, God will use other people to help sand down your rough edges and make you a better person. Be willing to learn.

3. Every person is going to have days when he is not really handsome or she is not incredibly beautiful. It's

okay to be attracted to someone's good looks, but if your relationship is not built on Christ and character, it will never last.

[LOVE VS. LUST:

WINNING THE BATTLE]

5 SIGNS A RELATIONSHIP IS
CENTERED ON THE LOVE OF GOD

When you first meet someone you are attracted to, there is usually a warm fuzzy feeling inside. Your heart pounds and maybe you even get goose bumps, but these feelings shouldn't be confused for God's love. You may have a "crush" or "puppy love." However, God's love is much deeper and more sincere.

Here are 5 signs to tell if you are in God's love.

1. You love the other person for who he or she is rather than what you get from the person. God freely gave us His Son with no strings attached. (John 3:16.)

2. You have Christ at the center of your relationship. (Matt. 6:33.) When Jesus is at the center of all you do, your conduct will never bring you shame or regret.

3. You are waiting until marriage for any physical relationship. Love is patient and willing to do what is right before God and best for the relationship. (1 Cor. 13:4.)

4. You respect the other person's feelings and wishes. Love never pushes someone to compromise what he or she believes is right. (1 Cor. 13:5.)

5. Love seeks to serve the other person rather than be served. (Phil. 2:3,4.)

Use these 5 benchmarks to measure your relationship to see whether it is built on God's love or human lust.

4 SIGNS A RELATIONSHIP IS LUST-CENTERED

Here are some signs you can look for in your relationships to see if you have strayed from God's kind of love to fleshly lust.

1. You look lustfully at the opposite sex. (Matt. 5:28.) This doesn't mean you can't look at the opposite sex in a decent manner. It's what you are thinking about as you do. If you couldn't look at the opposite sex, you would have to walk with your head down the rest of your life.

2. You're willing to compromise eternal rewards for short-term pleasure. (Heb. 12:16.) Take the path Moses did. He forsook the sinful pleasures of Egypt for the eternal reward from God. (Heb. 11:24,25.) The pleasure of sin lasts only for a season, but the reward of purity lasts forever.

3. You manipulate others to get what you want. "Baby, if you really loved me, you would prove it." If you really loved the person you said that to, you wouldn't ask him or her to compromise God's Word. The proof of love isn't physical; it's obeying God's Word and keeping Him at the center of your relationships.

4. You feel like you have to give in to the other person's pressure because you are afraid he or she won't love you if you don't. Perfect love casts out all fear. (1 John 4:18.) If your love is based on God's Word, you won't fear a human being. You will be more concerned about what God thinks than what anybody else thinks.

If you examine yourself against this checklist and find you are in lust instead of love, follow these steps.

1. Repent. (1 John 1:9.)

3. Renew your mind. (Rom. 12:2.)

4. Rebuild your relationship on God's Word.

4 WAYS TO AVOID SEXUAL TEMPTATION

You have probably seen someone mess up and make the excuse "the devil made me do it." This isn't a scriptural statement, because the devil can't make you do anything. He can only tempt you to sin. (Matt. 4:3.) You have to make the choice. Here are 4 choices you must make to help you avoid sexual temptation.

1. **Avoid the places of temptation.** (Rom. 13:14; 2 Tim. 2:22.) If you are around friends who feed you temptation, get new friends. If certain movies arouse temptation, change what you watch. Don't be alone with the opposite sex where you could be tempted. Stay in public.

2. **Purpose to remain pure.** (Dan. 1:8.) Daniel decided before temptation came that he would obey God's Word. You must decide up front to live pure. If you wait until you are in the middle of temptation, your resolve to do right will be weak.

3. **Hold yourself accountable to someone.** (Heb. 10:25.) Find a good spiritual friend who will encourage you in the things of God. When you know you

have to answer to someone about your actions, it
helps you stay on course.

4. **Be full of God's Word.** (Ps. 119:11.) God's Word is
your weapon to overcome temptation. Willpower alone
isn't enough. Jesus used Scriptures to overcome
temptation. (Matt. 4:1-11.) If you put God's Word in
your heart before the battle, it will come out in the
battle when you need it.

You can overcome sexual temptation if you carefully and diligently follow these practical steps.

7 SCRIPTURES TO ARM
YOUR HEART WITH PURITY

God's Word is called the sword of the spirit. (Eph. 6:17.) This is our main weapon to resist temptation. If you leave your sword at home, it can't help you in the battle in your daily life. The answer is what David did in Psalm 119:11. He put God's Word in his heart so it was there when he needed it. To help you do this, write down these 7 Scripture paraphrases on a 3 x 5 index card and carry it in your pocket. When you get a few moments throughout your day, pull these Scriptures out and memorize them so they will be in your heart when you need them.

1. **2 Timothy 2:22**: Flee youthful lusts.

2. **Ephesians 4:22-24**: Put off your old self; put on the new.

3. **2 Corinthians 5:17**: You are a new creation in Christ.

4. **Job 31:1**: Be careful what you watch.

5. **2 Peter 1:3**: He has given you everything you need. (You have a "need" for purity.)

6. **2 Corinthians 10:5**: Take every thought captive.

7. **Romans 13:14**: Make no provision for the flesh.

These Scriptures will help you walk in victory. Just as Jesus used Scripture to resist temptation and overcome, so can you. (Luke 4:1-13.)

3 IMPORTANT STEPS TO TAKE
IF YOU'VE SINNED SEXUALLY

If you have sinned sexually, it's important to realize that God isn't mad at you. Read the story in John 8:1-11 about how Jesus responded to the woman caught in adultery. He didn't condemn her. He forgave her and told her to go and sin no more. Don't be afraid to go to God like Adam and Eve, who hid from Him in the Garden. (Gen. 3:8.)

Here are 3 steps to help you get back on your feet if you have sinned sexually.

1. **Repent.** (1 John 1:9.) This means to do a 180-degree turn from the direction you were going. Notice, this verse says He will forgive and cleanse you.

2. **Reject condemnation from the devil.** The Holy Spirit never condemns; He only convicts. Condemnation is a feeling of hopelessness. Conviction is a stirring to repent and move forward in God. (Rom. 8:1-4.)

3. **Restore yourself spiritually by seeking godly counsel.** Find a spiritual leader in your life, such as a

parent, youth pastor, or youth leader you can confide in and receive godly counsel and encouragement from. (James 5:16; Prov. 28:13.)

Put these steps into practice, and you will be on course to recovery and to even greater spiritual heights than before.

[HAPPILY EVER AFTER]

5 REASONS TO MAINTAIN SEXUAL PURITY BEFORE MARRIAGE

The Bible instructs us to live a life free from sexual immorality. (Eph. 5:3; Col. 3:5; 1 Thess. 4:3.) However, God isn't trying to rob you of fun and pleasure. He has your best interest at heart. In fact, God created sex for our enjoyment as long as it is in the boundaries of marriage. (Heb. 13:4.)

Here are some of the reasons God instructed us to remain sexually pure before marriage.

1. **God protects us from a broken heart.** When you give yourself to someone sexually, you are giving that person your heart as well. If this person is not your spouse, then part of your emotions are in the hands of someone else. (1 Cor. 6:16.)

2. **God protects you from sexually transmitted disease and possible premature death.** (Rom. 1:27.) Every day young people die from AIDS. Not any of them ever thought it would happen to them.

3. **God protects your marriage from emotional baggage from the past.** You can be married to your spouse and have no guilt from past mistakes.

4. **God also helps you protect your self-esteem.**

5. **You are worth the wait.** If someone says he or she loves you but won't wait until marriage to have sex, then that person is lying. Love is patient. (1 Cor. 13:4.) You are worth waiting for.

Resist the temptation to give in to sexual pressure. God has your best in mind.

4 THINGS TO LOOK FOR IN A GREAT HUSBAND

Ladies, before you start thinking about marriage, you should know what is important to look for in a man. If you were shopping for a car, you wouldn't just buy the first one a salesperson pitched you. You would make sure it had the features you wanted. It's the same thing when looking at a relationship. You should know what is important. Just because a car looks great on the outside doesn't mean it runs. The same is true with guys. Just because they look good on the outside doesn't mean they have what is most important on the inside.

Here are 4 important things to look for in a potential husband.

1. **A strong spiritual leader.** You need a man who will spiritually lead you and be a pillar of faith and encouragement when life's storms come.

2. **A gentle spirit.** Life is too short to live with someone who is always angry and uptight. You want someone who is tender with words, not harsh.

3. **Deep character.** Ladies, you deserve a man who will love you and be faithful to you all the days of your life.

4. **One who respects you and your feelings.** A good indicator of how a young man will treat his wife is reflected in how he treats his mother. That is the way he will treat you.

Before you look for a husband, know what is really important. There may be more things than what I've listed here. Write them down and use them to measure potential relationships. If the traits are not in the person you really want, why waste your time dating him?

4 THINGS TO LOOK FOR IN A GREAT WIFE

Guys, there are a lot more things than looks to consider when searching for the right wife. The Bible says beauty is fleeting. (Prov. 31:30.) It is also what's *inside* that you must consider when building a relationship with a girl. That's what you will have to spend the rest of your life married to. Read Proverbs 31 for some good ideas on what to look for in a potential wife. Here are 4 good things to look for.

1. **Does she love God?** It is more important to have a wife who loves God than one who merely has passing beauty. I have a beautiful wife who loves God, but the thing I find most attractive about my wife is her love for God.

2. **Does she respect authority?** Look at how she treats her father. That is how she will one day treat her husband.

3. **Is she sexually pure?** You don't want a wife who will break your heart because she runs off with another man. When the honeymoon emotions are over, will she remain pure and devoted to you?

4. **Does she believe in you?** It's important to have a spouse who is supportive of your dreams. Life will throw enough negativity at you. You don't need to go home to a wife who doesn't believe in you.

There are probably more traits you want in a wife. Write them down and look at them when you are considering a potential relationship.

7 AREAS OF PREPARATION YOU MUST COMPLETE BEFORE YOU ARE MARRIED

Here are 7 important, but often overlooked, areas to work on before marriage.

1. **Spiritual stability.** Make a strong spiritual foundation in your life. This foundation will hold your life together through all storms. (Matt. 7:24-27.)

2. **Emotional health.** If you have emotional areas that aren't healthy, such as unforgiveness, unresolved anger, and severe mood swings, take this time before marriage to fix these.

3. **Physical fitness.** This will help you attract the opposite sex. It's true your future spouse should like you for what's inside, but he or she will also have to live with what's outside. Take care of your body, and your body will take care of you.

4. **Financial soundness.** Develop good responsibility with your money. Tithe, give, and save. Guys, women are attracted to someone they feel will be a good provider; it helps them feel secure. Ladies, guys are

frightened by reckless spenders; they are afraid they will never be able to satisfy your cravings for stuff. Be self-controlled and modest with your money.

5. **Maturity.** Be responsible in your actions. If you can't take care of yourself, how can you take care of a spouse and children?

6. **Friendship skills.** Learn to be a good friend. After all, marriage is spending the rest of your life with your best friend.

7. **Solving conflict.** Marriage will have conflicts and disagreements. The couples who last can solve differences with love and respect rather than sharp words and fighting.

Preparation time is never wasted time. The more you sweat in preparation, the less you bleed in battle.

6 HABITS YOU MUST ESTABLISH NOW IF YOU HOPE TO ENJOY A HAPPY MARRIAGE

The habits you form today determine the kind of life you live tomorrow. Someone once said, "First form your habits; then your habits will form you." What do you want to be? Form the habits, and your habit will help you achieve your goal.

If you want to attract a great mate, form these important habits.

1. **Patience.** The ability to be patient with others' faults will reap you the fruit of great friendship. What you sow, you reap. (Gal. 6:7.)

2. **Ability to listen.** This is a very important skill. No one wants to hang around someone who monopolizes every conversation. Ask what others think, and listen to them.

3. **Servanthood.** Marriage is a commitment to give your life to serve another. Learn this now, and it will be much easier when you get married.

4. **Humility.** This is the ability to say, "I was wrong; I'm sorry." Many marriages end in divorce because someone could not admit fault or apologize.

5. **Character.** This is the ability to stick to your commitment even when you don't feel like it. There will be many days when you won't feel like remaining married to your spouse, but character will see you through it.

6. **Love.** Read 1 Corinthians 13 for a good description of what real love is. This is the glue that holds a marriage together.

Form these habits, and you will be destined for a rewarding and fulfilling marriage.

ENDNOTES

[1] Maxwell, John. *The 21 Irrefutable Laws of Leadership.*
Nashville: Thomas Nelson, 1998.

ABOUT THE AUTHOR

Blaine Bartel founded Thrive Communications, an organization dedicated to serving those who shape the local church. He is also currently leading a new church launch in a growing area of north Dallas.

Bartel was the founding youth pastor and one of the key strategists in the creation of Oneighty®, which has become one of the most emulated youth ministries in the past decade reaching 2,500 – 3,000 students weekly under his leadership. In a tribute to the long term effects and influence of Blaine's leadership, hundreds of young people that grew up under his ministry are now serving in full time ministry themselves.

A recognized authority on the topics of youth ministry and successful parenting, Bartel is a bestselling author with 12 books published in 4 languages, and is the creator of Thrive-- one of the most listened to youth ministry development systems in the country, selling more than 100,000 audio tapes and cd's worldwide. He is one of the most sought after speakers in his field; more than one million people from over 40 countries have attended Blaine Bartel's live seminars or speaking engagements.

His work has been featured in major media including "The Washington Post," cbs' "The Early Show," "The 700 Club," "Seventeen" magazine, as well as newspapers, radio programs, and Internet media worldwide.

Bartel's commitment to creating an enduring legacy that will impact the world is surpassed only by his passion for family as a dedicated father of three children and a loving husband to his wife of more than 20 years, Cathy.

To contact Blaine Bartel,

write:

Blaine Bartel
Serving America's Future
P.O. Box 691923
Tulsa, OK 74169
www.blainebartel.com

*Please include your prayer requests
and comments when you write.*

To contact Oneighty®, write:
Oneighty®
P.O. Box 770
Tulsa, OK 74101
www.Oneighty.com

Take the Turn for God in Just 5 Minutes a Day

Witty, short, and inspiring devotions for teens from one of America's youth leadership specialists!

Teens can discover a real, action-packed, enthusiastic relationship with God. The thrive.teen.devotional is motivated by a very simple challenge: Give just five minutes a day to God and watch your life turn around.

At the end of eight weeks, the Word of God is going to be more real and alive to teens than ever before as they gain spiritual insights on issues like friendships, self-esteem, and prayer. The good news is that when one's mind is renewed, they experience a radical turnaround in every other area of their life, too.

thrive.teen.devotional
by Blaine Bartel
1-57794-777-0

OTHER BOOKS BY BLAINE BARTEL

every teenager's
Little Black Book
on reaching your dreams

every teenager's
Little Black Book
on how to get along with your parents

every teenager's
Little Black Book
of God's guarantees

every teenager's
Little Black Book
on how to win a friend to Christ

every teenager's
Little Black Book
for athletes

every teenager's
Little Black Book
on cash

every teenager's
Little Black Book
on cool

every teenager's
Little Black Book
of hard to find information

Little Black Book
for graduates

The Big Black Book
for parents

Let Me Tell You What
Your Teens Are Telling Me

Available at fine bookstores everywhere
or by visiting **www.harisonhouse.com**.

Harrison House
Tulsa, Oklahoma

PRAYER OF SALVATION

A born-again, committed relationship with God is the key to a victorious life. Jesus, the Son of God, laid down His life and rose again so that we could spend eternity with Him in heaven and experience His absolute best on earth. The Bible says, "For God so loved the world, that he gave his only begotten Son, that whosoever believeth in him should not perish, but have everlasting life" (John 3:16).

It is the will of God that everyone receive eternal salvation. The way to receive this salvation is to call upon the name of Jesus and confess Him as your Lord. The Bible says, "That if thou shalt confess with thy mouth the Lord Jesus, and shalt believe in thine heart that God hath raised him from the dead, thou shalt be saved. For whosoever shall call upon the name of the Lord shall be saved" (Romans 10:9,13).

Jesus has given salvation, healing, and countless benefits to all who call upon His name. These benefits can be yours if you receive Him into your heart by praying this prayer:

Heavenly Father, I come to You admitting that I am a sinner. Right now, I choose to turn away from sin, and I ask You to cleanse me of all

unrighteousness. I believe that Your Son, Jesus,
died on the cross to take away my sins. I also
believe that He rose again from the dead so that I
may be justified and made righteous through faith
in Him. I call upon the name of Jesus Christ to be
the Savior and Lord of my life. Jesus, I choose to
follow You, and I ask that You fill me with the
power of the Holy Spirit. I declare right now that I
am a born-again child of God. I am free from sin,
and full of the righteousness of God. I am saved
in Jesus' name, amen.

If you have prayed this prayer to receive Jesus Christ as your Savior, or if this book has changed your life, we would like to hear from you. Please write us at:

Harrison House Publishers
P.O. Box 35035
Tulsa, Oklahoma 74153

You can also visit us on the Web at
www.harrisonhouse.com